Original title:
Tying the Future

Copyright © 2025 Creative Arts Management OÜ
All rights reserved.

Author: Oliver Bennett
ISBN HARDBACK: 978-1-80586-106-5
ISBN PAPERBACK: 978-1-80586-578-0

A Stitch in Time

In a world of mixed-up seams,
Buttons fall from silly dreams.
Threading hope with laughs so bright,
We patch our days till stars ignite.

A needle dances in the air,
Stitching laughter everywhere.
With every tug, a giggle grows,
A fabric of joy in all our clothes.

Hopes Bound by Threads

With a twist and a playful yank,
Our aspirations join the prank.
Socks that no longer match are found,
In this patchwork joy, we're tightly bound.

A rainbow loop, a zany twirl,
All our wishes start to swirl.
Knotted dreams that make us grin,
Together, let the fun begin!

A Knot in Time

In the fabric of time, we tie,
A quirky sock that's flying high.
We tie our dreams with fraying ends,
Who knew that chaos could be friends?

A jolly knot with colors bright,
Keeps our futures in plain sight.
So let us trip with style and flair,
In this silly dance, we find our share!

Threads of Tomorrow

With threads spun from laughter's thread,
We weave a future, never dread.
A crazy quilt of hope and cheer,
We stitch together, year by year.

In these tangled yarns, we play,
Creating joy from every fray.
As we sew our dreams anew,
Tomorrow's bright with laughter too!

Weaving Dreams Ahead

In a loom of hopes we play,
Stitching laughter every day.
Patterns twist and twirl with glee,
Who knew yarn could set us free?

Grab your needles, don't be shy,
Let's create, you and I!
With every loop, we'll rise, we'll fall,
A tapestry that laughs at all.

The Fabric of What Comes Next

A patchwork quilt of bright desires,
Sewn together with silly wires.
Each square tells a quirky tale,
Of missing socks and fish that sail.

With fabric soft and colors bold,
We spin the stories yet untold.
Wrap your dreams, don't let them fray,
In our jolly fabric play.

Bonds Beyond Today

We're like spaghetti, tangled tight,
No sauce, just laughter, pure delight.
Our friendship's like a stretchy cord,
Bouncing back, never ignored.

Chasing joy, we skip and hop,
Running fast, we'll never stop.
Through thick and thin, we'll find our way,
Together gleeful, come what may.

Embracing the Unseen

Invisible threads tug at our hearts,
Binding mishaps with silly arts.
In the chaos, a dance unfolds,
A quirky script that never molds.

We twirl and swirl like dandelion fluff,
Building dreams with laughter, that's enough.
So let's jump into what's to be,
In this grand show of you and me!

Prophecies in Patterns

In squiggly lines, futures dance,
Mystic shapes in a humorous trance,
Worms in hats, they take a chance,
Giggling stars in their cosmic pants.

Clocks that melt and shoes that gleam,
They spin around like ice cream!
With every swirl, a quirky dream,
We're lost, it seems, in this wacky theme.

Crossroads of What's Ahead

At a fork, a chicken crows,
Waving flags of unknown prose,
One way leads to jelly beans,
The other's filled with rubber beans.

Should I don a clownish hat?
Or moonwalk with a playful cat?
The signposts giggle, twist, and shout,
As silly thoughts run carelessly out.

Tapestry of Change

Weaving threads of laughter bright,
Frogs in capes take flight at night,
Puppies dance with vibrant glee,
In this quilted tapestry.

Every patch tells a joke or two,
A banana peel, and here's a shoe,
As starlit giggles weave through time,
Turning woes into rhythms, sublime.

Fabric of an Unwritten Tale

On parchment skies, the ink is wet,
An octopus rides a bicycle pet,
Cats in glasses, quite posh they seem,
Writing a long-lost silly dream.

Whimsy threads that twist and twirl,
As robots dance and fairies whirl,
With every stitch, a punchline dropped,
An untold yarn, hilariously swapped.

Uniting Threads

In a world of mismatched socks,
We gather all our quirky clocks.
They tick and tock, a happy chime,
As we stumble through the sands of time.

A jumble of ideas, bright and bold,
We weave our tales, laughter uncontrolled.
With every stitch, a giggle's grown,
Together now, we're never alone.

Futures Interlaced

A hodgepodge of dreams, like jelly beans,
Sprinkle them with plans, or so it seems.
In a pot of ideas, we stir and sway,
Creating chaos in the funnest way.

With every mix, some may get stuck,
But who needs order? Let's test our luck!
With laughter as our guiding thread,
We'll wrap our hopes, and dance ahead.

The Uncharted Weave

In a loom of laughter, chaos reigns,
We stitch our hopes like runaway trains.
With colors bright and patterns wild,
We quilt our dreams, a joyful child.

And if a thread should snap one day,
We'll laugh it off, and find a way.
With needle in hand, we juggle and play,
Inventing futures, come what may.

Knots of Potential

We gather knots like tangled hair,
Making sense of this wild affair.
With every twist, a giggle shared,
In playful binds, we show we cared.

Each knot a tale of hopes untold,
In the fabric of life, we're brave and bold.
So tie your shoes, let's take a leap,
In knots of laughter, our joy runs deep.

The Unraveled Tomorrow

In a box of dreams, I found a shoe,
Only one, it bounced, oh what a view!
Chasing thoughts that run away,
I tripped on plans, or so they say.

A jigsaw puzzle's missing piece,
Found in my sock, oh what a tease!
Future laughs with every poke,
But here I am, just a silly bloke.

Fastening Aspirations

Socks on wrong feet, what a delight,
I ran a marathon... in my own fright!
With dreams like spaghetti, all twisty and twirled,
I danced with my visions, the future unfurled.

A yo-yo plan swings to and fro,
I'm juggling wishes, laughing, oh no!
Who knew a daydream could stick like glue?
A cat in a hat, now what will I do?

Emblem of the Unfolding

In the attic, I stumbled on a kite,
Wrapped in the past, what a weird sight!
Colors that whisper of joys yet to come,
With laughter and glee, it's never too dumb.

A recipe's missing, it calls for a laugh,
A pinch of nonsense, a quirky path!
With biscuits that giggle and skits on the run,
The emblem I carry, it's all in the fun.

Braiding Through Echoes

Echoes of laughter in the hallway,
I'm braiding my future, come what may!
A hat made of wishes, perched on my head,
Dreams spilling out like confetti bread.

I'm tying balloons to the hopes in my mind,
While squirrels critique, it's all so refined!
In the dance of the silly, I find my cue,
The future is bright, with a dash of me too!

Twists of Time

In a world where clocks all spin,
Cats wear hats while fish dive in.
Past and present play a game,
Running wild, they're all the same.

Jellybeans grow on rubber trees,
Dancing with the buzzing bees.
The future's wearing polka dots,
While we laugh at silly knots.

Wormholes wrap around the sun,
Chasing smiles, oh what fun!
Time-traveling with a twisty straw,
Sipping giggles, what a law!

So let's juggle all the years,
Swapping frowns for joyful cheers.
With a wink and a candy bar,
We'll find out just who we are.

Looming Change

Once a turtle raced a snail,
In a boat made out of kale.
Future's here, with socks to share,
Dancing while we brush our hair.

Socks and shoes begin to sing,
Hopping 'round like silly things.
Banana peels create a slide,
While we giggle, step aside!

Time's a balloon that floats away,
Full of helium, come what may.
Each tick-tock brings a silly grin,
Laughter echoing within.

Be it spaghetti or a dance,
Come and join the happy chance.
Adventures wait just down the street,
With every step, the future's sweet.

Quantum Connections

In a realm where wishes grow,
Bouncing on a rainbow's bow.
Particles dance, they tell a tale,
Of rubber ducks and flying snails.

Jumping jacks meet cupcakes, too,
With sprinkles dancing out of view.
Each quark giggles in delight,
As they frolic day and night.

Grains of sand hold dreams so vast,
Turning moments into blasts.
Beanies flying through the past,
Wondrous moments, oh so fast.

Entangled hearts make silly faces,
In a world of time and spaces.
Let's connect with joy combined,
And leave the worries far behind.

Bonds Beyond Time

Dancing through a kaleidoscope,
Finding visions, dreams, and hope.
Turtles wearing party hats,
Join a conga line of cats.

Echoes of a laugh today,
Chasing clouds that drift away.
Old jokes woven with new schemes,
As we fly on dancing beams.

Granite rocks that sing out loud,
Underneath a fluffy cloud.
Time becomes a slide to ride,
On a journey side by side.

Socks that squeak, and shoes that cheer,
Hold our bonds so very near.
With laughter's thread, we intertwine,
Creating joy that's truly fine.

Securing Tomorrow's Dream

In a land where wishes bloom,
We craft our hopes with a broom.
A lollipop tied to a kite,
We'll soar and giggle with delight.

With donuts on strings, we concoct,
Plans so sweet, they never get blocked.
Two squirrels dance in a trance,
As we tie our dreams with a chance.

Strings of Infinity

We'll knot our laughter in a bow,
While juggling dreams in a row.
Bananas tied to a bright balloon,
Flying high like a big cartoon.

In a world where socks go missing,
We'll fasten futures worth kissing.
With pickles in pockets, we'll roam,
Crafting a future that feels like home.

Bonds of Tomorrow

A rubber chicken for every plan,
We'll dance with glee like a silly clan.
Spinning donuts on invisible lines,
Making visions that sparkle and shine.

With bouncy castles made of dreams,
We'll slide into joy on fun's gleams.
Tying giggles with shoelaces long,
Singing a silly, playful song.

The Path Forward

On a pogo stick, we'll bounce ahead,
With marshmallow clouds as our bed.
Tying wishes like shoelaces tight,
We'll leap through tomorrow, what a sight!

With pancake hats on our heads,
We'll skip past worries like fluffy treads.
Adventurers with a wink and grin,
Crafting tomorrow, let the fun begin!

Threads of Potential

In a world so bright and quirky,
Threads of ideas dance like jerky.
With a twist and a turn, they spin,
Making futures where funny wins!

Laughter stitches every seam,
We're crafting a delightful dream.
Each loop a giggle, every knot
Creates the chaos we forgot!

Interwoven Fates

In a loom where mismatched socks stay,
Life's fabric stretches in a witty way.
With each stitch, we jive and sway,
Interwoven fates lead us astray!

A bumblebee zips, a cat did fall,
While weaving tales that tickle all.
With each knot a hearty chuckle,
We save sardines without the buckle!

Knots of Destiny

Tangled threads on a windy day,
Knots of laughter lead us to play.
Whether tangled up in humor or hair,
We find our way with a silly flair!

Oh the plans we weave with glee,
Like spaghetti in a crazy spree.
When one loop trips, the next one grins,
Dancing forward on life's whimsy sins!

The Weave of Dreams

In the loom of life, we take our stand,
Threading the oddities with a hand.
Each bizarre pattern brings us cheer,
The weave of dreams is strangely clear!

With vibrant colors, we boldly twirl,
Creating a tapestry that gives a whirl.
Tickle my fancies, make me beam,
In our quirky fabric of a shared dream!

Echoes of What Lies Ahead

In a world of magic beans,
Where dreams wear silly jeans,
We juggle futures, three in tow,
While our pet goldfish learns to sow.

Time travels on a pogo stick,
Bouncing over clocks so quick,
With cheese hats and jelly shoes,
We slide away from yesterday's hues.

Our plans are made on a whim,
Like a dance with a singing brim,
Laughing as we launch our kite,
Skimming on clouds with pure delight.

Each giggle whispers tales anew,
Painting skies in every hue,
So pack your bags, let's misbehave,
As we await what tomorrow gave.

Linking the Unknown

With rubber bands and bubblegum,
We stitch the future, oh so fun!
A recipe for laughter bold,
Mixing dreams with tales untold.

In a world where cats wear ties,
And genius squirrels rule the skies,
We paint our hopes with crayon bright,
Crafting joy from sheer delight.

We're surfing waves of plastic fries,
With seagulls dressed in clever guise,
While our gadgets dance and sing,
Connecting us to everything.

So raise a toast with fizzy drinks,
And let your imagination wink,
For adventures wait on every block,
As we unite our funny flock.

Footsteps into Infinity

We tiptoe on banana peels,
As laughter spins the crazy wheels,
A march of ducks, a jazzy tune,
While space monkeys zoom past the moon.

In tick-tock shoes, we prance about,
Twisting futures like a sprout,
With umbrellas made for sunny days,
And marshmallow clouds in a sugary haze.

Each step echoes with giggles clear,
As we dance through every cheer,
Jumping hurdles made of cheese,
And fending off the ticklish breeze.

Chasing shadows of what could be,
We weave our joy so easily,
With silly hats and wobbly moves,
Our rhythm sets the path that grooves.

The Convergence of Dreams

In a circus of bright pastel,
Our dreams collide, ring the bell!
We juggle hopes like jellybeans,
Creating future's wacky scenes.

A chorus of giggles fills the air,
As starlit llamas strut with flair,
Unicorns sashay in the breeze,
While singing rhymes with utmost ease.

We launch our wishes like paper planes,
And catch them back in sunny rains,
With every swoop, a chuckle grows,
For life's best tales are spun in prose.

So join the dance with lemon pies,
As we eat dessert and touch the skies,
In this madcap world, we weave with glee,
Uniting dreams eternally.

Binding Threads of Time

In a world where socks mismatched,
I chase my dreams with flair and snatch.
When life hands me a tangled kite,
I laugh and soar, oh what a sight!

If time's a ball of yarn to twist,
I'll knit my whims, you can't resist.
A sweater made of silly hopes,
With sleeves that sport wobbly ropes.

I tie my shoelaces with a grin,
For every stumble, I just spin.
The future's like a jiggly jell,
I poke and prod, it bounces well!

So grab your thread and join my spree,
We'll weave a tale of pure jubilee.
In this quirky loom of fate,
We'll dance and laugh, oh isn't that great!

The Fabric of Tomorrow's Journey

With buttons made of dreams, we sew,
A patchwork quilt where giggles flow.
Stitching rainbows, bright and bold,
In every corner, stories told.

A fabric shop of wobbly fun,
Where mishaps shine like summer sun.
I throw a dart at plans with glee,
The future's fabric, wild and free!

We'll thread our worries with a smile,
Each stitch a step, oh what a style!
With every tug, we stretch and roam,
In this colorful world, we craft our home.

So let's unravel all the strife,
And weave a tapestry of life.
With silly patterns, we'll design,
A splendid fabric, yours and mine!

Sculpting Paths to Possibility

I carve my dreams with cookie dough,
A sprinkle here, a twist there, whoa!
With frosting paths that lead the way,
To chase the crumbs of bright today.

In gardens full of jellybeans,
I plant my hopes in wobbly scenes.
Each lollipop a future treat,
I taste the fun, oh what a feat!

With a rubber mallet of delight,
I sculpt my fate, it sparkles bright.
A whimsical wonderland, I see,
Where laughter grows like a tall tree.

So break the mold and join the cheer,
In this zany dance, we have no fear.
Crafting dreams with giggly grace,
Together, let's embrace the chase!

Ribbons of Destiny

In a world spun high with laughter,
We dance with dreams, light as air.
Balloons filled with hopes and chatter,
Each one a wish, just floating there.

With shoelaces tied in silly bows,
We leap through puddles, no care to spare.
Mirrors reflecting jolly prose,
Our fate is stitched in cheeky flair.

Grapes in hats on a picnic spread,
Silly faces made without dread.
We juggle our plans, a life widespread,
Awaiting the cake, topped with shred.

So grab a string, let's weave a tale,
With laughter's thread, we'll never fail.
Through every twist and every trail,
Our joyful knots will always prevail.

The Path We Create

With crayons held in tiny hands,
We map our dreams on paper lands.
Odd shapes tumble, bright and grand,
In every line, joy expands.

Skipping stones on a wobbly stream,
Waves of giggles, burst of steam.
We write our paths, a wild theme,
While sporting socks that don't quite seam.

Lemonade stands and ice cream cones,
Silly hats and wobbly phones.
Our crooked steps create new zones,
In this adventure, serious tones.

So let's adorn our zany flight,
With sparkly stars and pure delight.
Each step we take, a silly sight,
Together we'll shine, forever bright.

Interlocking Wishes

With paper clips and a sunny smile,
We latch our dreams in crazy style.
Each wish we make, a playful trial,
As puzzle pieces waltz a while.

In mismatched socks, we laugh and play,
Building castles that sway and sway.
With sticky notes, we'll find a way,
To string our thoughts in a dreamy array.

Cupcakes stacked like shiny towers,
Countless sprinkles, sugary flours.
We weave our fate with tiny powers,
As joy blooms bright in colorful showers.

So come along, let's intertwine,
Our playful dreams will brightly shine.
With every giggle, life's divine,
In this mad dance, we feel so fine.

Nest of Dreams

In a cozy nook with pillows round,
We gather our wishes, safe and sound.
Dreams like popcorn, goofily bound,
In this soft nest, joy is found.

With mustache straws in cups of cheer,
We sip on giggles, spread the gear.
Each silly tale, we hold so dear,
A world of whimsy, ever near.

Fortress made of blankets snug,
We snicker softly, give a shrug.
Pillow fights, where we dance and chug,
Our dreams unfurl like a sweet bug.

So let's nest in colors bright,
With laughter echoing, pure delight.
In this haven, every night,
We craft our dreams, a charming sight.

Threads of Tomorrow

In a world where socks roam free,
I chase them down with glee.
A twisty fate awaits the lace,
As mismatched hopes we all embrace.

Pants and shirts form a parade,
Dancing bright in sunlight's shade.
With every spin, a laugh we share,
Life's tangled yarns lead us somewhere.

Knots of Destiny

I tied my shoes with dreams afoot,
But stumbled twice, look, who'd have thought?
A bow that knows how to misbehave,
    Leads me to the oddest rave.

With every knot, a tale unwinds,
Silly moments, the best of finds.
No need to fret, just let them roll,
These playful ties that make me whole.

Weaving Dreams Ahead

In the loom of life, threads do play,
We stitch our goals in a goofy way.
Fuzzy strands tied in a spazz,
Creating patterns with a pizzazz.

A tapestry of laughter hangs,
Woven tightly with funny pangs.
Critique my art? Oh, please be kind,
This masterpiece is one of a kind!

Boundless Horizons

With expectations stretched like old tights,
We leap into the silliest sights.
A jump, a skip, and whoops, a fall,
But what a ride! We love it all.

Flying kites on a windy spree,
Chasing clouds and wild jubilee.
Horizons call with a wink and grin,
Let's tie it all with a joyful spin!

Boundless Threads Ahead

In a world where socks just disappear,
We chase the lint like a hilarious spear.
With mismatched shoes, we strut with glee,
Fashion's a riot, just wait and see.

Unruly hairdos to match our flair,
Every morning's a bold affair.
Mixing patterns, oh what a scene,
The more absurd, the more we beam.

With spaghetti noodles as our guides,
We twirl through life with rainbow strides.
A dance of colors, laughter in tow,
The future's bright, just follow the glow.

Let's weave our hopes with silly yarn,
A tapestry of dreams where we're never worn.
With every stitch, a chuckle we send,
Each goofy knot binds us 'til the end.

Unfolding Visions

In a land where cats wear tiny hats,
And dogs recite the news like sprightly spats.
We sketch our plans with crayons bright,
Silly drawings bring delight in sight.

Doodles of cupcakes, and rainbows bold,
A future that's quirky, never old.
We leap through puddles of jelly beans,
In a world of wonders, as odd as dreams.

With ticklish feathers that dance and sway,
Our wild ambitions lead us astray.
Yet here we giggle, in swirls of mirth,
Crafting our whims, with unbounded worth.

So join the fun, hang on tight,
Through cosmic mischief, we sail in flight.
With laughter as our compass, joy in command,
We'll navigate this zany land.

Yarn of Tomorrow

In the attic sits yarn with a mind of its own,
Knitting goofy scarves, all brightly shone.
We tangle ourselves in a vibrant spree,
Creating styles that almost flee.

With every stitch, a new tale starts,
A penguin wearing sneakers wins our hearts.
Llama-shaped hats and sweaters too,
In the land of whimsy where absurdities grew.

We'll wrap the clouds in fluffy threads,
A blanket cozy where laughter spreads.
Sailing on dreams that come in spins,
Crafting a future with grins and grins.

So let's unravel what life may send,
With every loop, we'll just pretend.
The future's a ball of yarn, oh so fun,
Let's stitch our stories, the chance has begun.

The Gathering of Intentions

At the gathering, silliness prevails,
With oversized glasses and painted trails.
We toast with fruit punch, cheers oh so loud,
In a fest where oddballs seem so proud.

Here, wishes float like balloons on a string,
We chase them down, oh what joy they bring.
A parade of dreams, in festive attire,
Marching to rhythms that never tire.

With giggles and hope, we make our plans,
Building towers of cookies with gooey hands.
Our shared intentions, like stars above,
Spark with laughter, and a sprinkle of love.

This tapestry woven with care and delight,
Supports our tomorrows with kindness and light.
Join the dance, let your dreams take flight,
In this gathering, everything feels right.

The Stitch of Possibilities

With needles sharp and fabric bright,
We sew our dreams, oh what a sight!
A patchwork quilt from hopes we weave,
In every stitch, a tale to believe.

A cat jumps in, oh no, what fun!
The yarn rolls away, the chaos begun.
Twisting and turning, we laugh all night,
Creating a future that feels just right.

Threads of laughter in colors bold,
We dance around, our tales retold.
Each loop and knot, a whimsical flair,
In this silly tapestry, we lay bare.

So gather 'round, let's start to play,
With every stitch, we'll find our way.
In a world of fabric, so wild and free,
We find our joy, just you and me.

Knotted Paths to Tomorrow

Two shoelaces tangled, what a sight,
One's pulling left, the other, right,
With every step, we trip and fall,
A comedy show, we're having a ball!

The map is drawn in crayon and cheer,
A route so zigzagged, it's perfectly clear.
A squirrel scoffs as he darts past us,
In this playful chaos, there's no need for fuss.

We jump through hoops, and over the moon,
With cartwheels and giggles, we'll iron this tune.
Our paths may twist like pretzels undone,
But together, my friend, we'll have lots of fun!

So let's embrace the knots on the way,
They're just surprises for us to play.
With each little laugh, we make our mark,
In this hilarious journey, we spark the dark.

Interlacing Horizons

Two colors merge in a swirl of cheer,
Your orange goes with my sky-blue here.
With crayons stretched to their very ends,
We sketch a world where laughter bends.

The horizon winks with a funny smirk,
As clouds grab coffee and put in some work.
Chasing rainbows with our socks mismatched,
In the game of life, we're all attached!

With a twist and a turn, the shape's all wrong,
But who said that shaping should take long?
We'll twirl and spin till the sun says 'hi',
In our interlaced dance, we'll reach the sky.

So let's paint our dreams on this canvas bright,
With dips and flips, until it feels right.
Horizons blend in a giggling spree,
In this charming chaos, just you and me.

Loom of Change

Come gather round the loom of fun,
With threads so bright, we've only begun.
A little nudge and a cheeky grin,
We'll weave our tales and let them spin.

With each new loop, there's a giggle to find,
A roll of yarn that's perfectly blind.
It hops and skips like a froggy dance,
In this silly fabric, we take our chance.

The weaver chuckles as colors clash,
In this magical mess, we create a splash.
A hopscotch dream made of cloth and cheer,
We'll cut the strings and watch them veer.

So let's embrace the mess, my friend,
For laughter and yarn don't have an end.
In this loom of mischief, let's arrange,
A wacky world, a beautifully strange.

Cord of Destiny

Like spaghetti on a plate,
We twist and turn with fate.
Each noodle a dream, it seems,
A pasta party of our schemes.

Let's tie our shoes and start to race,
With laces flying, what a pace!
But watch your step, oh please do try,
Or you'll trip on dreams and fly!

We're bound by fate, a curious thread,
With every giggle, joy's widespread.
A knot, a loop, a tangled cheer,
So let's embrace this life, my dear!

In the end, it's quite absurd,
Our plans may fall, we're never heard.
But laughter's the cord that intertwines,
In this jester's dance of silly signs.

The Future Befriended

In a world where dreams wear hats,
And you can hear them chatting rats.
We'll walk our dogs through time and space,
Winking at each funny face.

Jumping over puddles of tomorrow,
Dodging all those old woes and sorrow.
With cake in hand, oh what a treat,
Life's a funny dance on happy feet!

Let's paint the skies with rainbow hues,
With smiles that chase away the blues.
We'll shout our plans, both bold and nutty,
As we giggle through the world's cuddly.

Oh friendship binds us, what a score,
Together we'll explore, explore!
So here's to the laughs we've yet to brew,
The future's bright, it's all for you!

Sails Set Towards Tomorrow

With sails of paper and dreams galore,
We drift from shore, and then explore.
In a boat made of chocolate fudge,
We sail on giggles, not a grudge.

Wind in our hair, we feel so spry,
Laughing with clouds as they float by.
Every wave's a joke, no doubt,
With fish that dance and flouts about.

Maps drawn in crayon, all askew,
Lead us to treasure, yes, it's true!
Nuts and berries we'll call our gold,
In this thief of laughter, we are bold.

So hoist those sails, let's ride the tide,
With laughter as a faithful guide.
Toward tomorrow, in a nutty boat,
We'll find our path, and steer, and gloat!

Paths Intertwined

Two roads met in a whimsical place,
With a giggle, they began to race.
One wore flip-flops, the other boots,
A dance of paths in silly suits.

Chasing sunbeams, they spun around,
Twirling dreams that leap and bound.
With every step, a joke is spun,
Life's a party—come join the fun!

A squirrel yelled, "Hey, what about me?"
As he fluffed his tail, climbing a tree.
Paths crossed like noodles in a bowl,
Making music, blending soul to soul.

The journey's ridiculous, filled with quirks,
Twisting time like crazy smirks.
Together we'll dance till day is done,
For life's a giggle, let's share the fun!

Bridges to New Beginnings

Across the river, ducks have a chat,
While squirrels plan the next acrobat.
With sticks and leaves, they build a great span,
To link the next meal from a faraway can.

Bicycles zoom, puncturing the day,
With helmets that wobble in a quirky way.
Each step we take, the bridge bends and groans,
As laughter echoes in silly tones.

Joggers in tights with a silly grimace,
Try to keep up in the silly race.
Their shoes are bright, like candy in stacks,
As they fly over bridges, with giggles and quacks.

Pigeons coo softly, crafting their plot,
To snatch all the crumbs each runner forgot.
Together they gather, a feathery crowd,
While the bridge shakes beneath—oh how wild and loud!

The Interwoven Journey

Two socks together, a mismatched pair,
Hopping through life without a care.
Laces tangled in a playful dance,
They trip over puddles, in a splashy romance.

Road trips planned with snacks galore,
In a car that's held up by dreams and more.
Maps flipped upside-down, GPS on strike,
Yet every wrong turn feels just like a hike.

Funky hats fly, adorned with flair,
The wind gives a twist to our unkempt hair.
Each unexpected stop, a giddy delight,
As we laugh 'til it's dark—what a silly sight!

With every bump, we tattoo a tale,
Each hiccup a laugh, every chuckle a grail.
Together we mingle, a tapestry spun,
In this woven journey, we're never done!

Merging Streams of Time

In puddles of dreams, ducks float and play,
As moments collide in their quirky ballet.
The clock is a tick-tock with hiccups and spins,
While time plays hopscotch, and laughter begins.

Silly old clocks with faces so round,
Laugh at the moments swirling around.
With a wink and a nudge, they keep us on track,
As we chase the hours, never looking back.

Marshmallow clouds drift lazily by,
While time jumps on pogo sticks—oh my!
With each bouncing giggle, a giggly twist,
As time and our joys weave a riotous mist.

Life's a blender, a swirl and a whirl,
In the chaos, we giggle, let laughter unfurl.
As moments merge into laughter sublime,
In our goofy escape through the rivers of time!

Anchors of Hope

A ship in the harbor with dreams in its sails,
Anchors the laughter wherever it hails.
We dance on the decks, all hands in the air,
As waves tickle toes without a care.

Nautical maps, with doodles and strife,
Rescue plans drawn in the circle of life.
Each splash is a giggle, each trip is a jest,
For who needs a compass when you're having the best?

Sea monsters chuckle as they peek through the blue,
"Come join the party!" They sing and they coo.
With octopus arms waving wildly about,
We gather our hope, there's never a doubt.

Through storms and through laughs, we'll sail with delight,
Waving to the wind, through day and through night.
Our anchors hold firm, with humor as rope,
In this raucous adventure, we float on with hope!

Tethered to Tomorrow

In a world where dreams take flight,
We tripped on shoelaces, what a sight!
With hats askew and smiles wide,
We float through clouds, our laughter's guide.

Balloons tied tight to our old bikes,
We ride past squirrels, avoiding spikes.
With jellybeans in pockets deep,
We bounce through puddles, no time for sleep.

Ties of Hope

A rubber band wraps 'round my brain,
It stretches far, won't break in vain.
My coffee spills, yet I don't care,
Tomorrow's chaos, I'll boldly dare.

With a wink and a nudge, we leap,
Into the unknown, our laughter deep.
A dance of chance, two left feet,
In our pockets, candy treats meet.

The Loom of After

We weave our plans with silly string,
In every mishap, joy we bring.
Each knot a story, tangled tight,
We giggle loud, and what a sight!

With mismatched socks and hats so bright,
We prance around, hearts full of light.
Stitching laughter into our seams,
We embroider life with wacky dreams.

Bridging Now and Beyond

We build a bridge of marshmallow,
With gummy bears and a jello flow.
Balancing snacks, we take a chance,
Each step we take, a silly dance.

As we reach the other side,
We trip on giggles, let joy be our guide.
In whimsical worlds where laughter reigns,
We skip through life, shedding all chains.

The Knot of Promise

In a world of silly aims,
We tie our dreams like shoelace games.
A twist, a pull, a comical plight,
As visions dance in joyful light.

With every knot, a giggle's born,
Like tying socks on a unicorn.
Plans flop and flip, a merry whir,
While laughter echoes, "What's the blur?"

We promise fate with quirky schemes,
Like juggling pies or silly screams.
A knot that binds our lives so bright,
In frothy dreams that take their flight.

So grab some yarn, let's weave a tale,
Where futures twist and never pale.
With laughter high and spirits free,
We knot our hopes—just you and me!

Spinning Tomorrow

Watch the wheel spin, round and round,
Tomorrow's charm in laughter's sound.
With every turn, a ticklish jest,
As we chase dreams with cheeky zest.

Like cats on yarn, we tumble and roll,
Crafting laughter to soothe the soul.
Calamity strikes with every throw,
Yet in our chaos, joy will grow.

Plans may wobble, or go astray,
But chuckles guide us all the way.
Each silly twist, a joke we share,
As futures spin in playful air.

So let's embrace this wacky dance,
With mismatched socks and a daring chance.
In our spinning world, we'll always find,
A comical way to be entwined!

The Fusion of Yesterdays and Tomorrows

In a blender of giggles, we mix our days,
Yesterday's memories in humorous ways.
A splash of the past, a sprinkle of cheer,
As we whirl into laughter, without any fear.

Mixing old woes with tomorrow's dreams,
A recipe crafted with silly beams.
We skewer regrets on a cocktail stick,
And toss in some joy for a funny flick.

Time's a jigsaw with pieces askew,
Where past and now create something new.
So let's stir our fate, with a wink and a grin,
And toast to the chaos that's held within!

In the blender of life, we dance and spin,
Taking past blunders and turning them thin.
Together we share this whimsical song,
A fusion of time where we all belong!

Embracing the Threads of Time

Stitching moments with threads of glee,
We patch our lives just you and me.
With needle and laughter, we sew and spin,
Each snip and poke, a chuckle within.

Time laughs with us, a playful seam,
Winds of humor in every dream.
We patch the rips with quirky flair,
Embracing the oddities, so rare!

Every frayed end has a tale to tell,
Like mismatched socks in a whimsical spell.
We tie up our jokes, with zany delight,
As we dance through the day and into the night.

So grab that thread, let's weave our rhyme,
With quirky patterns in the fabric of time.
In stitches and giggles, we'll bask and shine,
Embracing all threads—it's perfectly fine!

The Weaving of Wishes

In a loom of dreams, we twist and turn,
With each wild thought, our hopes all burn.
A squirrel jumps in, adding flair,
As we weave our fate with a chuckling air.

A tangled yarn may tickle your nose,
While giggling clouds wear funny clothes.
Stitching up laughter, we craft our schemes,
On a fabric of folly, where whimsy gleams.

Sails set for Tomorrow

We set our sails with a wink and grin,
Chasing the breeze, let the fun begin!
A parrot squawks with a pirate's glee,
While jellyfish dance in the shimmering sea.

A compass spins, yet we don't fret,
For adventures await, with no regret.
With laughter as wind, we dash through waves,
On a ship made of dreams where mischief behaves.

Threads of Anticipation

A needle of hope stitches day by day,
With patterns of joy that lead us astray.
As cats chase yarns, we laugh at the chase,
Creating a world that's a funny place.

With every twist, a joke to unfold,
In a tapestry bright, our stories told.
We hop on the thread of unforeseen cheer,
As we dance through life, with a skip and a leer.

Interlaced Futures

In a jigsaw of time, we piece with delight,
Crafting our paths, oh what a sight!
A rubber chicken joins in the fun,
As we mix our dreams, like moon and sun.

With colors so bright, and laughter so loud,
We dance hand in hand, a whimsical crowd.
Our futures entwined in a playful embrace,
With every giggle, we quicken our pace.

Aligning the Stars

The stars had a meeting, quite late at night,
They danced and twinkled, what a silly sight.
They argued on planets, the best place to roam,
Yet all agreed Earth felt just like home.

One claimed it was Mars, with its red dusty charm,
Others laughed loudly, 'It's way too warm!'
They plotted a course for adventure and fun,
Spaceships made of cookies, oh, how they run!

The moon served as waiter, serving stardust treats,
Galactic comedians cracking up all the beats.
With laughter and laughter, they shaped their own fate,
In cosmic confusion, they simply can't wait.

So if you look skyward, and giggle a bit,
Remember those stars and their cosmic skit.
Tangled in laughter, and silly delights,
Dreams swirl and spin in the vast starry nights.

Webbing Future Paths

In the garden of choices, we plant silly seeds,
We water with laughter, and pull out the weeds.
Each path we concoct, isn't smooth, oh no,
But who needs a map when you're ready to go?

Kites carried us high, with strings made of dreams,
Chasing after rainbows, or so it seems.
We danced through the chaos with socks that don't match,
Each step an adventure, life's wildest patch!

Caterpillars caught in a web of pure fun,
Chasing butterflies makes the world come undone.
Sticky notes whisper, 'Let's paint the town bright!',
With paintbrushes waving, we flirt with delight.

So stumble and giggle, as you dance on your way,
Each misstep a giggle, come join in the play.
In this tangled webbing, we craft what we choose,
Tomorrow's a party, so let's never lose!

A Tapestry of Hope

Weaving in colors, vibrant and bold,
Each thread tells a story, each story unfolds.
The loom of our dreams is a sight to behold,
With laughter as needle, and joy as our mold.

A whimsical dance of our thoughts intertwined,
We gather our quirks, and leave troubles behind.
Patchwork of giggles, and zany designs,
Each knot holds a secret, as silly as pines.

Threads twist and twirl, creating a scene,
Weathered and wild, like a romping raccoon.
Embroidered with kindness, stitched close with a smile,
Each patch tells us, let's stay for a while.

So hang up your tapestry, let it shine bright,
A quilt of tomorrow, made warm by delight.
In every odd corner, a tale will awake,
Woven with humor, for laughter's own sake.

Moments Entwined

In a garden of tickles, we play hide and seek,
Each moment we share makes our laughter peak.
With whimsies that tumble, and giggles that swirl,
Time's wiggly fingers give each day a twirl.

We skated on dreams, on ice made of fun,
Racing through clouds, under the ticklish sun.
Pacifiers for puppies, and popcorn for cats,
In this mixed-up world, we wear wiggly hats.

Moments entwined like spaghetti on spoons,
With wishes that sail like inflatable balloons.
Jumping in puddles, making splashes and glee,
Each giggle a treasure, in memories we see.

So grab all the moments, don't let them disguise,
With a sprinkle of laughter, watch joy rise.
Entwined we shall dance, with no map to find,
In this zany adventure, we're joyfully blind.

Tying the Present

In a world where socks go to roam,
They've formed a club, far from home.
Gone on adventures, it's quite a scene,
Rescue them quick, they're lost and keen.

Lunch breaks are not for just a bite,
But planning escapes, oh what a sight!
With coffee and donuts, they stall the grind,
Spreading the joy, leaving stress behind.

Interwoven Journeys

The cat's in the hat; oh what a spree,
Chasing his tail, he's lost what to be.
Unraveling yarn in a delightful mess,
Turned into a scarf, oh what a stress!

Two squirrels debated, who'd bury the nut,
Danced round the trees, then fell with a thud.
They laughed, then they argued, with nuts in their cheeks,

A comedy show for the tree-hugging geeks.

Pathways in Motion

Worms in a race, who'd take the prize?
They wriggled and giggled, oh what a surprise!
With every squirm, they forged new tracks,
Tripping on soil, in nature's snacks.

While time ticks away, the ants march in line,
Balancing crumbs, seeking breakfast divine.
Yet slipped on a puddle, those tiny brigade,
Made a splash party, oh what a parade!

Unraveling Futures

Bubble gum dreams in silly balloon,
They floated so high, over fields in bloom.
Chasing the clouds, while dodging the rain,
They giggled and popped, in joy and in pain.

A hedgehog on skates, what a strange sight,
Rolling down hills, oh what pure delight!
Yet tangled in weeds, took a moment to pause,
With laughter and love, found the best cause.

Unfurling Dreams

In the garden of hopes I do frolic,
Chasing sunbeams, oh, how symbolic.
Each daisy a wish, blooming so bright,
I'll swim in the clouds until night.

With a kite made of pizza, I soar high,
My laughter's the fuel as I touch the sky.
A squirrel, my co-pilot, eats all my snacks,
Together we plot, no chance of relax!

Building castles of giggles with ease,
In the kingdom of nonsense, I reign as I please.
The future's a clown, with shoes far too big,
Stepping on dreams, doing a jig.

With jellybean bridges and sprites made of fluff,
I leap over puddles, both joyful and tough.
So come join my circus, don't wait too long,
We'll dance through the chaos, our lives a sweet song.

Untying Potential

Once a tortoise dreamed of speed, oh so clever,
He plotted his course, determined forever.
With shoelace rockets, he zoomed down the lane,
Making his foes rethink the race game.

A cat wearing glasses, studying the skies,
Invents a new gadget that captures the flies.
He proudly proclaims it with utmost delight,
"Let's patent this magic, let's get it right!"

The future's like jello, a wobbly treat,
We dance through the flavors, a sugar rush feat.
With sprinkles of laughter, we toast to the day,
Unraveling potential, in our zany way.

So grab a balloon, let's float far and wide,
With unicorns dancing and rainbows as guides.
Together we'll chase what the day has in store,
With whimsical plans, oh, we always want more!

Threads of Ambition

A spider spins tales in corners of dreams,
Weaving up plans with glittery seams.
Each thread a giggle, each knot a new cheer,
In this web of ambition, we'll conquer our fear.

The rabbits in bow ties, all polished and neat,
Hold a summit for veggies, it's quite the retreat.
With carrots for badges and peas for the rank,
Together they plot in their leafy green tank.

A giraffe with a scarf, looking quite dapper,
Wonders who'll join him for tea and a caper.
In a world full of colors, both vivid and bright,
We tackle each challenge with sheer delight.

So pull on your sneakers and join on this ride,
With dreams interwoven, we won't be denied.
The future is funny, let's laugh as we grow,
On a rollercoaster of wishes, come on, let's go!

Forging New Links

In a factory of laughter, we crank out some dreams,
With gears made of giggles and jolly extremes.
Polka-dotted robots dance in a line,
Sculpting our futures, all shiny and fine.

A walrus in socks, leading the crew,
Whistles a tune as they build something new.
With hammers of laughter and nails made of fun,
Together they forge a bright place for each one.

The cupcakes are singing, the sprinkles are bold,
As they plot a new venture that never gets old.
In this bakery of joy, with frosting as glue,
We'll serve up our visions, all fresh and brand new.

So grab a confetti and climb on this ride,
Join the parade of enchantment with pride.
The links we are forging aren't heavy, you see,
Just ribbons of whimsy, wild and carefree.

The Loom of Possibilities

In the workshop of dreams, we play,
Spinning yarns of tomorrow, come what may.
With a wink and a nod, we twist the threads,
Creating futures where laughter spreads.

We pluck at the strings of wishes and schemes,
Frolicking in fields of wild, silly dreams.
Every loop a giggle, each knot a grin,
As we dance on the loom, let the fun begin!

Our patterns are quirky, a colorful mess,
Like socks that don't match, we just say 'yes'.
We stitch up the moments, mischievous flair,
And wear our zany futures like a vibrant hair!

So join in the fun, let's weave and frolic,
With each twist and turn, life's a grand frolic.
In the loom of our laughs, who knows what will bloom,
As we craft a tomorrow that dances in the room!

Weaving a New Dawn

When morning breaks with a sparkle and cheer,
We grab our old looms and bring them near.
With each clank and click, we find our beat,
Making patterns of pancakes and colorful treats.

A dash of the silly, a sprinkle of spice,
Creating the fabric of fate that's quite nice.
We tie in some humor, a stitch full of fun,
And laugh as we shine like the bright, rising sun.

The threads may be tangled, a comical sight,
But oh the joy in setting things right!
We'll weave tales of whimsy, of cats in a tree,
Where every new dawn holds a grand jubilee!

So throw in the yarn, let the mischief ensue,
For in our great weaving, there's fun just for you.
As we craft this new dawn, with giggles abound,
We'll laugh at the threads of the life we have found!

The Intersections of Time

At the crossroads of whens, a signpost appears,
Pointing to futures, stirring up cheers.
With each tick of the clock, we jive and sway,
Dancing through moments, oh what a delay!

Past loves and mishaps, they meet for a chat,
Sharing the stories of this and of that.
With a wink at the present and nod to the past,
The laughter echoes, it's a time that won't last.

We weave through the seconds, in funny old shoes,
Chasing the seconds, we can't seem to lose.
"Wait for me, time!" we giggle and shout,
As we race toward futures, all twisting about.

So come join the fun, let's romp through this space,
Where the intersections of time hold a whimsical grace.
With each precious moment, we'll dance and unwind,
In this hopscotch of life, leave the worries behind!

Horizon's Embrace

As the sun kisses shore with a flick and a flair,
We gather our dreams, tossing them in the air.
With a giggle and sparkle, we make our own way,
Creating a horizon where we laugh and play.

Adventure awaits, with each wave that rolls,
We'll surf on our dreams, like giddy young souls.
With sand in our toes and joy in our hearts,
We'll build up our futures like playful old arts.

The embrace of tomorrow is wild and absurd,
Like a kite in the sky with a very odd word.
"Fly high!" we'll whisper, with a chuckle and cheer,
As we soar toward horizons, we hold dear!

So grab your sun hats, let's dance in the sun,
With laughter and love, our journey's begun.
In the arms of the future, so bright and so free,
We'll giggle through life like a honeybee!

Stitched Promises

In a world of mismatched socks,
Where dreams dangle like a fox,
We stitch the seams with laughter bright,
And dance beneath the neon light.

A button here, a patch there,
We giggle in this threadbare wear,
With every stitch, a promise made,
In quirky patterns, fears allayed.

So let's embroider what we crave,
With silly tales that we will save,
For every knot and every seam,
We'll tie together this wild dream.

In whimsical loops, our hearts do play,
As fabric sways in a cheerful way,
So grab that yarn and weave with cheer,
Our silly future, crystal clear.

Embracing the Unwritten

With inkblots splashed in chaos wide,
We pen our tales with gusto, pride,
Each word a wink, each phrase a grin,
In pages blank, our dreams begin.

The tales unscripted twist and turn,
Like spaghetti while we laugh and yearn,
For every plot that goes awry,
We're scribbling jokes with a sly eye.

A coffee spill, a doodle spree,
Unplanned fun is where we'll be,
So grab your pen, let's scribble bold,
In this mad book, let's break the mold.

Stories dance, and laughter rings,
In drafts of silliness, joy springs,
With every laugh, a new line flows,
Our quirky future, in letters grows.

The Pathway of Bonds

On a pathway paved with jelly beans,
We skip along, in crazy scenes,
With every step, our laughter echoes,
As friendship blooms like many meadows.

A breadcrumb trail of silly pranks,
With goofy hats and mischievous flanks,
We hop along like bouncy balls,
In this funny dance, no one wants falls.

Side by side in playful glee,
With bonds as stretchy as a rubber tree,
We leap through puddles, hearts aglow,
On this wobbly path, we steal the show.

Together we weave through giggles and grins,
In this parade where each laughter wins,
So take my hand, and let us roam,
For in each bond, we make a home.

Knotted Visions

In a world where thoughts get tangled up,
Like pretzels tossed in a wobbly cup,
We twist our dreams in silly guise,
With knots of laughter, joys arise.

Each vision's twist could trip a clown,
But with each stumble, we won't frown,
We'll hop and skip through twisted lines,
In this whimsical maze, joy shines.

Our plans may swirl in a messy dance,
Yet in this chaos, we find romance,
For every knot, a tale to weave,
In laughs and giggles, we believe.

So let's embrace these tangled schemes,
In funny hues, we chase our dreams,
With knotted visions tied with cheer,
Our silly journey's crystal clear.

The Fabric of What's Next

Threads are weaving, colors collide,
Socks on the left, shoes take a ride.
Future's a party, balloons in a row,
Cleaning the house? No way, let it glow!

Silly designs that nobody chose,
Hats made of fruit, and socks with a nose.
Jumping ahead like a clown on a stage,
Life's just a comic, turn the next page!

We're crafting our dreams from leftovers true,
Pasta for breakfast, who knew it could brew?
Future's a canvas, splashes of glee,
Dare to get funky, just wait and see!

Laughter's the fabric that holds it all tight,
Doodles in margins, fun takes its flight.
So let's stitch together absurdity's charm,
In this zany quilt, you'll find your own arm!

Knots in Time

Tangled in laughter, we trip on a shoe,
A future that giggles, just me and you.
Knots on the dance floor, we spin and we sway,
Caught in a loop, come what may!

Pants that are too big, let's dance with no care,
Who needs a plan when there's snacks everywhere?
Future's a puzzle with pieces so bright,
Let's toss them around like confetti in flight.

Climbing up charts with spaghetti for ropes,
Riding on dreams like unruly little hopes.
Twists in our paths lead to versions so bold,
Let's laugh at the strays that we left in the fold.

Bending the rules with a wink and a laugh,
Crafting a story that leads to our path.
So tie up your shoelaces, let's take a wild ride,
With knots in our journey, we'll glide side by side!

Tapestry of Possibilities

Weaving a quilt from the quirkiest dreams,
Milkshakes for breakfast, no matter the themes.
Colors are jumbled, a misfit parade,
This tapestry giggles; let laughter invade!

Patterns are shifting, and what will we find?
A dinosaur wearing a hat that's entwined?
Dust bunnies dancing to their own little tune,
Under the glow of a million bright moons.

Frogs in top hats serve tea with a twist,
Knitting up futures from the quirkiest list.
Pulling at threads with a giggle and cheer,
Life's such a carnival, let's give it a sneer!

So spread out the fabric, let colors unfurl,
In this funny world, give a wink and a twirl.
With every new patch and every wild scene,
The tapestry's crazy, but oh-so-keen!

Anchored Aspirations

Sailing on dreams with a rubber duck fleet,
Goals that are sticky like gum on your feet.
A compass that spins in a whimsical way,
Riding the waves of serendipity's play.

Anchors are donuts, getting us stuck,
But who needs a map when you're rolling in luck?
The horizon's a joke with a twist on the side,
Navigating nonsense, let's enjoy the ride!

Juggling our hopes with a pie in the sky,
A future of ice cream, oh my, oh my!
With every big splash, we're dancing around,
Anchored in laughter, let joy be unbound.

So hoist up our sails, let the laughter abound,
In ships made of whimsy, we've all been crowned.
With frosting-lined dreams and a balloon full of cheer,
Our anchored ambitions are silly but clear!

www.ingramcontent.com/pod-product-compliance
Lightning Source LLC
Chambersburg PA
CBHW060112230426
43661CB00003B/163